CLASS 150 SPRINTERS

Andrew Cole

AMBERLEY

First published 2020

Amberley Publishing
The Hill, Stroud
Gloucestershire, GL5 4EP

www.amberley-books.com

Copyright © Andrew Cole, 2020

The right of Andrew Cole to be identified as
the Author of this work has been asserted in
accordance with the Copyrights, Designs and
Patents Act 1988.

ISBN 978 1 4456 8207 5 (print)
ISBN 978 1 4456 8208 2 (ebook)

British Library Cataloguing in Publication Data.
A catalogue record for this book is available from
the British Library.

Typesetting by Aura Technology and Software
Services, India. Printed in the UK.

Introduction

The Class 150 units can trace their way back to the start of the 1980s. At that time, British Rail still retained a large fleet of first-generation blue square DMUs, which were starting to become unreliable and in need of costly overhaul. It was decided to build a new fleet of modern units in order to replace the older stock.

Two different designs were introduced: the low-cost Class 142–144 Pacer units that were used on shorter distance services, and Class 150 Sprinter units that were to be used on longer distance services.

The Class 150 units were based on the British Rail Mk III design, having similar body profiles and a ribbed roof. In 1984 the first of two prototype units was released from BREL at York. Numbered 150001, it was fitted with Cummins power units and Voith gearboxes. It was soon followed by the second prototype, No. 150002, but this differed in having Perkins engines, with automatic gearboxes supplied by the Self Changing Gear Company.

The two prototype units were delivered as three-car units, and were to be the only sets to have a purpose-built centre car, which they still have today. No. 150002 would prove to be the more unreliable of the two, and so it was decided to upgrade it as a test bed for the upcoming Class 158. One car was fitted out with a new Class 158 interior, and it was fitted with Cummins power units. While it was in this configuration it was renumbered, firstly to 154001, then as 154002. When its role as test bed was over, it reverted to a standard Class 150 unit, regaining its previous identity.

A total of fifty Class 150 units would follow the two prototypes off the production line at York, numbered 150101–150150. All were painted in Provincial livery, and would be based at Derby Etches Park depot. Following the introduction of new-build units, they would be concentrated on Tyseley for commuter workings in the West Midlands, and also Newton Heath for the same purpose in Manchester. They were built without gangway doors on the front, retaining a flat appearance.

Tyseley would receive the first thirty-two of the Class 150/1 units for use in the West Midlands. A total of eight units would eventually pass to Silverlink on privatisation, with the West Midland fleet operated by Central Trains. Some would also be transferred to Great Western, including the Silverlink examples. When London Midland replaced Central Trains as the holder of the West Midlands franchise, they ordered Class 172 units to replace the remaining Class 150/1 units, with the majority passing to Northern Rail, leaving just three sets in Birmingham to work Bedford–Bletchley and also Hereford services.

Eventually the remaining First Great Western examples and the three remaining London Midland examples joined the rest of the Class 150/1 fleet at Newton Heath.

At the end of 1986 the first of another batch of Class 150 units left BREL York. No. 150201 was the first of eighty-five units that were built in a slightly different design to the first batch; most notably, they were fitted with through gangway doors on the cab front, but they were also fitted with a power-operated crew door rather than a slam door.

The class was mainly delivered to Newton Heath and Neville Hill depots, but some were also allocated to Haymarket and Cardiff Central. This sub-class was to be transferred between various depots, far more than the original batch. Ten were to find their way to Norwich for use on Anglian lines; these later passed to Central Trains in exchange for Class 156 units. A total of eighteen were to find use north of the border in Scotland; they would be replaced by Class 170 units, and all would be transferred to Cardiff Canton.

Some of the Central Trains sets would be disbanded, and the sets split and inserted onto Class 150/1 units to create a three-car set. This had been done previously by Regional Railways, but when the Class 172 units were introduced by London Midland, the sets were returned to their original formations, and transferred to Northern Rail.

Many of the Class 150/2 units have carried names, with most of the Anglian fleet, as well as the Wessex Trains fleet, which were later absorbed into First Great Western, carrying them. The Silverlink Class 150/1 units also received nameplates.

Today the Class 150/2 units are operated by three different franchises: Transport for Wales has the biggest number, followed by Northern and Great Western Railway. Only the Transport for Wales units are scheduled for replacement, and this by 2023. Two Class 150/2 cars have been scrapped following collision damage, with the two remaining serviceable cars forming a new unit.

An extra Class 150/1 unit was produced, solely for the purpose of track recording, passing to the British Rail Board at Derby. It can now be found working for Network Rail with the set number 950001.

Both batches are formed of DMS(L) + DMS cars, with the DMS(L) being numbered 52101–52150 and 52201–52285; the DMS cars are numbered 57101–57150 and 57201–57285. The two prototype cars are slightly different, being DMS(L) + MS + DMS, with the cars numbered 55200/01 + 55400/01 + 55300/01.

I hope you enjoy looking through my collection of Class 150 photographs, which show an unsung workhorse both of British Rail, and also post-privatisation. The units are set to be around for a few more years yet, as most are now compliant with PRM (People with Restricted Mobility) features.

No. 150001, 20 July 1987

No. 150001 is seen working past Saltley Depot, Birmingham. In this view the unit is three years old, and it was a regular performer in and out of New Street. It was built as a prototype unit, hence the non-driving centre car, one of only two in the Class 150 fleet.

No. 150001, 18 June 2019

No. 150001 is seen over thirty years after the previous photograph. In this view the unit now carries Great Western Railway green livery, and is currently based at St Philip's Marsh Depot, Bristol. A move to Northern is on the cards for this unit.

No. 150002, 13 April 1985

No. 150002 is seen arriving at Derby. This was the second of the two prototype units, also being delivered as a three-car unit. No. 150002 was powered by a Perkins engine, but this would be changed to a Cummins engine to match the rest of the fleet.

No. 150002, 3 July 2017

No. 150002 departs from Bristol Temple Meads with a Great Western Railway working to Frome. The two prototype units still retain their non-driving centre cars, making them unique in the Class 150 fleet.

No. 150003, 29 June 2006

No. 150003 is seen making a station call at Birmingham Moor Street. This unit carries Regional Railways Centro livery as it was based in the West Midlands at the time. The unit was reclassified as a Class 150/0 due to the extra Class 150/2 car inserted in the middle, in this case car No. 57210 from unit No. 150210.

No. 150004, 7 August 2007

No. 150004 is seen at Rugeley Trent Valley carrying full Central Trains livery. The Class 150 units were used on the Chase Line in the West Midlands, from Walsall through to Stafford via Cannock. This unit is supplemented with car No. 52216 from No. 150216, making it a Class 150/0.

No. 150007, 1 November 2007

No. 150007 is also seen at Rugeley Trent Valley carrying unbranded Central Trains livery. The franchise had been taken over by Govia at this point, and the services were now operated under the London Midland name. No. 150007 operated with car No. 52202 from unit No. 150202 in the centre.

No. 150010, 15 January 1995

No. 150010 is seen stabled on Tyseley Depot carrying Regional Railways Centro livery. The Class 150 units were synonymous with Tyseley until the last set was transferred to Northern in 2019. No. 150010 is seen with car No. 57226, in the centre, from unit No. 150226.

No. 150011, 27 October 2005

No. 150011 arrives at Birmingham Snow Hill carrying Regional Railways Centro livery. The class was heavily used on the lines operating out of Snow Hill until replaced by Class 172 units. No. 150011 has car No. 52206 from unit No. 150206 in the centre.

No. 150018, 24 September 2005

No. 150018 is seen at Bournville on Birmingham's Cross City line. Despite the route being electrified, on this day the line was operated as far as Bournville by diesel Class 150 units due to engineering work. No. 150018 is seen running with car No. 52220 from unit No. 150220 in the centre.

No. 150101, 3 July 2017

No. 150101 is seen at Bristol Temple Meads carrying First Great Western livery. It had worked in from Weymouth, and would soon be transferred north to Northern along with the rest of the Great Western fleet.

Nos 150102 and 150101, 2 August 1986

Nos 150102 and 150101 are seen stabled side by side on Tyseley carriage sidings. In this view, the units had not long been in service, and both carry Provincial livery, which suited the class well.

No. 150102, 21 May 2019

No. 150102 is seen at Manchester Victoria carrying the latest Northern white livery. All the Class 150/1 units are now operated by Northern, and are all based at Newton Heath, Manchester.

No. 150103, 10 March 2015

No. 150103 is seen departing from Manchester Piccadilly. This unit carries the livery of the former operator of the Northern franchise, Northern Rail, not to be confused with the current operator, Northern. This unit was transferred north when it had been displaced in the West Midlands.

No. 150104, 20 May 1996

No. 150104 is seen at Chester with a working to Birmingham New Street. This unit carries Regional Railways Centro livery, and was a bit outside of its normal operating area, deputising for a Class 156 or a Class 158.

No. 150104, 13 August 2013

No. 150104 is seen at Cardiff Central with a First Great Western Railway working to Exeter St David's. The operating sphere for the FGW units was massive, from Worcester in the north all the way down to Penzance.

No. 150105, 22 February 1986

No. 150105 is seen when not very old at Tyseley carriage sidings, carrying Provincial livery. The class was introduced to help eliminate first-generation blue square DMUs from longer distance routes in and around the Midlands.

No. 150106, 21 May 2019

No. 150106 departs from Manchester Victoria with a Northern working to Leeds. The unit carries former First Great Western blue livery, but with the logos removed. The class is currently being fitted with new disabled access facilities to enable the units to be used from 2020 onwards.

No. 150107, 22 May 2016

No. 150107 passes through Kidderminster with an empty stock working to Worcester. The unit carries full London Midland livery, one of only three units to do so. The three sets have since moved to Northern.

No. 150107, 21 May 2019

No. 150107 is seen under the magnificent roof of Manchester Piccadilly. As can be seen, the unit still retains its former London Midland livery, but with the logos crudely masked out. It will eventually receive Northern white livery.

No. 150108, 13 August 2013

No. 150108 arrives at Bristol Temple Meads with a First Great Western working to Weston-super-Mare. The unit is seen coupled with a Class 153 single car.

No. 150109, 18 October 2016

No. 150109 is seen near Proofhouse Junction on the approaches to Birmingham New Street. The three London Midland units were used both on Marston Vale services from Bedford to Bletchley and on Hereford services from New Street.

No. 150110, 7 December 1985

No. 150110 is seen along with a classmate at Tyseley carriage sidings. As can be seen from the destination blind reading 'Bangor', when operated by Provincial the units were used far and wide. A Class 104 unit can be seen alongside; the Class 150s helped eliminate the Class 104s from service.

No. 150111, 13 April 2016

No. 150111 is seen departing from Manchester Piccadilly with a Northern working to Chester. This was another unit inherited from London Midland.

No. 150112, 16 June 2017

No. 150112 arrives at Manchester Victoria with a Northern working to Wigan Wallgate. The class is heavily used on services through Manchester Victoria, with a good selection to be seen there throughout the day.

No. 150113, 7 December 1985

No. 150113 is seen stabled on Tyseley carriage sidings carrying Provincial livery. As can be seen, units in the class were delivered without deflector plates on the front, these being fitted later.

No. 150114, 17 February 1991

No. 150114 stands inside the factory at Tyseley undergoing repairs. The unit carries Regional Railways Centro livery for workings in the West Midlands area.

No. 150115, 13 April 2016

No. 150115 departs from Manchester Piccadilly with a Northern service to Hazel Grove. By this time the franchise was operated by Northern, but most of the units still carried the old Northern Rail livery.

No. 150116, 14 October 1990

No. 150116 is seen at Tyseley carriage sidings. This unit was the first member of the class to carry Regional Railways Centro livery and had just been released from works. The livery was a radical departure from the Provincial livery previously carried.

No. 150116, 4 June 2013

No. 150116 departs from Sheffield with a Northern Rail working to Leeds. The class works far and wide working for Northern and can be seen at almost any point of the Northern network.

No. 150117, 22 February 2017

No. 150117 is seen arriving at Platform 14 at Manchester Piccadilly with a Northern Rail working to Blackpool North. Today these services are in the hands of Class 319 electric units, following the electrification through to Blackpool.

No. 150118, 10 March 2015

No. 150118 is seen at Manchester Piccadilly, waiting to depart for New Mills Central. Even following refurbishment, the Class 150/1 units still retain their roller destination blinds rather than having electronic ones.

No. 150119, 10 March 2015

No. 150119 stands on the buffer stops at Leeds station, waiting to depart for Manchester Victoria. With such a large fleet of units, any type of unit can appear on any Northern working.

No. 150120, 26 December 1994

No. 150120 is seen in the depot yard at Tyseley. The unit is seen carrying Regional Railways Centro livery, but also has Regional Railways branding applied. This would be one of the Class 150 units that passed to Silverlink and it would gain the name *Gospel Oak – Barking 2000* in 2004.

No. 150120, 9 July 2016

No. 150120 departs from the delightful station at Bodmin Parkway. The unit is seen carrying First Great Western livery and is heading for Penzance. This is the interchange station for the Bodmin & Wenford Steam Railway.

No. 150121, 22 May 2008

No. 150121 arrives at Bristol Temple Meads. The unit can be seen carrying former Silverlink livery, but with the logos removed and large First Great Western ones applied. No. 150121 was named *Willesden Eight* when in Silverlink use.

No. 150122, 21 May 2019

No. 150122 is seen waiting to depart from Manchester Oxford Road with a Northern working to Manchester Airport. Northern inherited quite a large number of Class 150 units from First Great Western and put them into service before repainting or refurbishing them.

No. 150123, 12 May 2004

No. 150123 is seen at Bletchley, waiting to depart for Bedford. No. 150123 carries Silverlink livery and also the name *Bletchley Seven*. It is one of three names this unit has carried, the other two being *Richard Crane* and *Willesden TMD*. The Silverlink units were used on the Marston Vale line and also on the Gospel Oak to Barking line in London.

No. 150123, 7 September 2004

No. 150123 *Bletchley Seven* arrives at Barking in East London. There were seven units in the Silverlink fleet at the time, but No. 150121 arrived soon after, and they were replaced by new Class 172/0 units, which in turn have now been replaced with Class 710/2 electric units.

No. 150124, 27 October 2005

No. 150124 is seen departing from Birmingham Snow Hill for Worcester. The unit carries Regional Railways Centro livery, but this would be replaced with Central Trains livery.

No. 150124, 23 May 2007

No. 150124 waits departure time and the signal at Rugeley Trent Valley with a Central Trains working to Stafford. There would only be a further six months' operation of the Central Trains franchise, with London Midland taking over in November 2007.

No. 150124, 3 July 2017

No. 150124 is seen at Bristol Temple Meads after arriving from Weymouth. It was soon transferred to Northern following the reallocation of First Great Western Class 166 units to the Bristol area.

No. 150126, 11 January 1986

No. 150126 is seen stabled in the carriage sidings at Tyseley. When new, all fifty members of the class were regularly found in the Birmingham area until the last eighteen were transferred up to Newton Heath.

No. 150126, 14 January 2007

No. 150126 is seen shunting around the depot at Tyseley. At the time, this was the last Class 150 to carry Regional Railways Centro livery, and it would soon be repainted into the Network West Midlands livery.

No. 150127, 9 July 2016

No. 150127 is seen awaiting departure time at Exeter St David's with a First Great Western working to Exmouth. Today, FGW has only the two prototype Class 150/0 units on its books, but they too are scheduled to move to Northern, following the rest of the class. No. 150127 came to FGW from Silverlink, where it was named *Bletchley TMD*.

No. 150128, 9 July 2016

No. 150128 is seen stabled on the depot at Exeter. At the time, First Great Western operated sixteen Class 150/1 units, along with four three-car units, two of which were made up of hybrid sets. This set carried two different names while in Silverlink service: *Community Forest* and then *Bedford – Bamberg 30*.

No. 150129, 22 February 1986

No. 150129 is seen stabled at Tyseley carriage sidings amongst various first-generation units. Note the Class 116 centre car alongside, No. 59631, which still retained plain blue livery. No. 150129 would later pass to Silverlink, where it was named *Marston Vale*.

No. 150129, 13 January 2016

No. 150129 departs from Bristol Temple Meads with a First Great Western working to Gloucester. Note how this unit now carries the large name *Devon and Cornwall Rail Partnership*.

No. 150130, 3 November 2017

No. 150130 is seen at Bristol Temple Meads, waiting to depart for Cardiff Central. This unit was also named, being *Severnside Community Rail Partnership*, but this was the third name that it had carried; when in Silverlink service it carried the names *Bedford – Bletchley 150*, and then *Bletchley Pride*.

No. 150131, 14 April 2016

No. 150131 departs from Bristol Temple Meads with a First Great Western working to Cardiff Central. At the time, part of the FGW fleet was allocated to St Philip's Marsh, Bristol, and the remainder at Exeter. This unit once carried the name *Leslie Crabbe* when it was in service with Silverlink.

No. 150132, 17 March 1998

No. 150132 passes through an unkempt Water Orton carrying Regional Railways Centro livery and heading for Gloucester. This was taken during the early days of Central Trains, when there hadn't been too much livery change.

No. 150132, 26 May 2008

No. 150132 is seen at Hednesford on Birmingham's Chase Line. This unit is seen carrying Network West Midlands livery, which was only carried by a small handful of units.

Nos 150132 and 150201, 16 June 2017

Nos 150132 and 150201 are seen side by side at Manchester Piccadilly. This view illustrates perfectly the main difference between the two sub-classes: the front gangway doors on the later units, which provided access from one unit to another when running in multiple.

No. 150133, 10 March 2015

No. 150133 departs from Leeds with a Northern Rail working to Morecambe. It is seen coupled with single-car Class 153 No. 153378. No. 150133 was previously in service with Silverlink and carried the name *Northern Star*.

No. 150134, 27 August 1997

No. 150134 arrives at a very wet Preston with a terminating service. This unit carries Regional Railways North Western livery: black and grey with a white and red stripe.

No. 150135, 16 July 1986

No. 150135 is seen, most unusually, on Lawley Street Freightliner terminal, Birmingham. The reason for this visit is unknown, but the class did have a parcels area at one end of the unit, where the seats tipped up to create a large space.

No. 150135, 20 May 1996

No. 150135 is seen at Chester, waiting to depart for Wigan. This unit is seen carrying Regional Railways North Western livery, which suited the class well.

No. 150136, 22 April 1996

No. 150136 is seen disappearing into one of the tunnels at Liverpool Lime Street with a working to Morecambe. The final eighteen members of the class were allocated to Newton Heath for local workings in the North West.

No. 150136, 12 June 2008

No. 150136 is seen departing from Manchester Piccadilly, having been repainted into Northern Rail livery. The unit is heading for Buxton, an area which has been associated with the class for many years.

No. 150137, 14 March 1987

No. 150137 is seen on the fuel pumps at Tyseley carriage sidings, carrying Provincial livery. It is surrounded by first-generation blue square units, which the Class 150s helped start to eliminate from the West Midlands.

No. 150137, 13 February 2016

No. 150137 is seen arriving at Manchester Piccadilly with a terminating service. It is coupled with Class 156 No. 156440, both carrying Northern Rail livery, as a Class 390 departs for London Euston.

No. 150138, 30 December 2016

No. 150138 is seen having arrived at Manchester Victoria with a terminating service. Despite carrying Northern Rail livery, this was now operated by new owner Northern.

No. 150139, 9 June 1996

No. 150139 is seen at the delightful station at Buxton. It carries Regional Railways North Western livery, and is seen waiting to depart for Blackpool North.

No. 150139, 1 July 2017

No. 150139 is seen on the buffer stops at Liverpool Lime Street, along with a Northern Class 142 and a London Midland Class 350.

No. 150140, 22 February 1991

No. 150140 passes Washwood Heath, running in a hybrid livery of both Provincial and Sprinter livery. It was two cars from two different units coupled together to make a serviceable set.

No. 150140, 19 October 2007

No. 150140 departs from Manchester Piccadilly, heading for the nearby Manchester Airport. The unit is seen carrying former First North Western stars livery, but has had Northern branding applied. It had been three years since First Group ran the franchise, so repaints were not exactly quick.

No. 150141, 22 February 2017

No. 150141 is seen arriving at Manchester Victoria, carrying Northern Rail livery. It had been on a relatively short run to Stalybridge.

No. 150142, 26 December 1988

No. 150142 is seen stabled on Tyseley carriage sidings, carrying Sprinter livery. This livery was applied new to Class 150/2, Class 155 and Class 156 units, and a few of the Class 150 sets also received it.

No. 150143, 21 May 2019

No. 150143 departs from Manchester Piccadilly, carrying the new Northern white livery. This had been through Wabtec at Doncaster for a full refurbishment, including many new PRM (People with Restricted Mobility) modifications.

No. 150144, 16 February 1997

No. 150144 is seen at Stafford carrying Sprinter livery. The individual side numbers on this car were a lot larger than normal and it was the only car to carry this size numbers, making it easily recognisable.

No. 150144, 26 May 1998

No. 150144 departs from Chester, heading for Liverpool Lime Street, while carrying Sprinter livery. This view clearly shows the larger than normal side numbers carried by this car.

No. 150145, 9 May 2000

No. 150145 is seen having arrived at Buxton with a terminating service. This unit is seen carrying First North Western stars livery, which looked plain and dated in this view.

No. 150146, 26 December 1989

No. 150146 spends Christmas 1989 stabled on Tyseley carriage sidings. As can be seen, this unit has been made up to a three-car train with the addition of car No. 52252 from set No. 150252.

No. 150146, 21 September 1995

No. 150146 departs from Manchester Piccadilly, heading for Buxton, having been returned to its original formation. This unit is seen carrying Regional Railways livery, a livery not carried by many members of the class.

No. 150146, 24 June 2008

No. 150146 is seen waiting to depart from Manchester Victoria. The unit now carries Northern Rail livery, but has had decals added to the centre depicting Liverpool as the City of Culture in 2008.

No. 150147, 6 September 1986

No. 150147 is seen stabled at Tyseley carriage sidings when still relatively new. Note the Class 128 parcels unit to the right, one of three which were allocated to Tyseley for Express Parcels work.

No. 150148, 16 July 2013

No. 150148 is seen arriving at Leeds carrying Northern Rail livery. This side of the station is where the old parcels bays used to be, but it was redeveloped to give extra platform space at this very busy station.

No. 150149, 9 December 1989

No. 150149 is seen on Tyseley Depot. This has been split from its sister vehicle in readiness for a Class 150/2 car to be inserted to make it a three-car set. The units were never renumbered when running as three-car sets, unlike today, where they would have been.

No. 150149, 21 September 1995

No. 150149 departs from Manchester Piccadilly with a service to Buxton. By this time the unit had been returned to its normal formation and still carries Sprinter livery but, unusually, the lower part of the front of the unit has been painted black.

No. 150149, 1 April 2008

No. 150149 is seen at Liverpool Lime Street carrying the former First North Western stars livery. It had been four years since First Group stopped running the franchise, and this was the last Class 150/1 unit to carry this livery.

No. 150150, 26 July 1986

No. 150150 is seen stabled on Tyseley carriage sidings along with a classmate. This was the final member of the Class 150/1 units to be delivered, and all fifty were delivered carrying Provincial livery.

No. 150201, 20 May 1996

No. 150201 is seen at Chester, waiting to depart for Southport. This was the first Class 150/2 delivered, and it is seen carrying Regional Railways Merseyrail livery.

No. 150202, 14 April 2016

No. 150202 is seen at Bristol Temple Meads, waiting to depart for Cardiff Central. The unit carries First Great Western blue livery, but this car has no branding, just the First Group logo. This unit was inherited from London Midland.

Nos 150203 and 150139, 9 June 1996

Nos 150203 and 150139 are seen side by side at Buxton. The two units carry different Regional Railways liveries, No. 150203 carrying Merseyrail and No. 150139 carrying North Western. The Class 150 units have always been regular visitors to Buxton, and still are today.

No. 150203, 17 January 2008

No. 150203 is seen at Manchester Piccadilly with a Northern Rail working to Manchester Airport. It would soon lose its former First North Western livery in favour of Northern Rail livery.

No. 150204, 17 February 1991

No. 150204 is seen on Tyseley Depot, having just returned from works overhaul and repainting into Regional Railways Centro livery. This set would be disbanded to make up a couple of three-car formations, with the cars inserted into Class 150 sets Nos 150112 and 150114 to create Class 150/0 units.

No. 150205, 13 February 2016

No. 150205 is seen departing from Manchester Piccadilly. Northern Rail applied many different vinyls to its fleet of Class 150 units, and No. 150205 carries 'Welcome to Yorkshire' adverts. The addition certainly brightened up the units.

No. 150206, 25 October 2017

No. 150206 is seen stabled at York. This was another unit inherited from London Midland when it introduced Class 172 units. No. 150206 carries the latest Northern livery, one that is spreading fast among the Northern fleet.

No. 150207, 20 March 1988

No. 150207 is seen at Sheffield carrying Sprinter livery. The Class 150/2 units were all introduced carrying this livery, and some were delivered with the grey extended around the front and the yellow just on the gangway doors, but these were soon repainted. No. 150207 has since left the North West and is now based at Exeter, working for Great Western Railway.

No. 150208, 4 November 2018

No. 150208 is seen making a station call at Cardiff Queen Street. The Class 150/2s have always been associated with South Wales, but units have transferred in and out of the area. No. 150208 carries former Arriva Trains Wales livery, but it is now operated by Transport for Wales.

No. 150209, 21 May 2019

No. 150209 is seen at Manchester Victoria. This set is made up from the two surviving cars from two withdrawn Class 150/2 units, Nos 57209 and 57212. With both cars being Driving Motor Standards, there are no toilet facilities on board, so it normally operates with a Class 153, in this case No. 153331.

No. 150210, 22 February 2017

No. 150210 is seen arriving at Manchester Piccadilly with a Northern working to Blackpool North. When used by London Midland, this set was disbanded twice and the cars used as centre vehicles in Class 150/0 units, firstly Nos 150117 and 150118, then Nos 150105 and 150103.

No. 150211, 12 June 2008

No. 150211 departs from Manchester Piccadilly, heading for the airport. With such a sizeable fleet of Class 150s, Piccadilly and Victoria are great places to see them in action.

No. 150213, 12 May 2001

No. 150213 is seen on the buffer stops at Lowestoft. Anglia had a small fleet of ten Class 150/2 units, but they were exchanged with Central Trains Class 156 units, with one transferring to Arriva Trains Wales. No. 150213 carries the name *Lord Nelson*.

No. 150214, 30 December 2016

No. 150214 is seen in the dark confines of Manchester Victoria, looking a little grubby in its former Northern Rail livery.

No. 150215, 22 February 2017

No. 150215 is seen having arrived at Manchester Victoria with a terminating service. This is another member of the class to carry 'Welcome to Yorkshire' adverts on its former Northern Rail livery.

No. 150216, 14 April 2016

No. 150216 departs from Bristol Temple Meads carrying First Great Western livery. Another former London Midland example, this unit is heading for Bristol Parkway. FGW has a fleet of twenty Class 150/2s in service.

No. 150217, 30 July 2016

No. 150217 makes a station call at Lydney with an Arriva Trains Wales working to Cheltenham Spa. This was the later version of ATW livery, replacing the blue and white livery. When this unit was operated by Anglia, it carried the name *Oliver Cromwell*.

No. 150218, 21 April 1996

No. 150218 stands at Crewe carrying Regional Railways North Western livery, and is waiting to depart for Chester. Upon leaving the station, the train will bear left and go past Crewe Electric Depot and Crewe Works.

No. 150219, 3 July 2017

No. 150219 is seen arriving at Bristol Temple Meads carrying First Great Western blue livery. The unit has a very clean yellow end, having been through works for collision repairs after it had collided with Class 43 No. 43160 at Plymouth.

No. 150220, 13 April 2016

No. 150220 departs from Manchester Piccadilly with a Northern working to Hazel Grove. These workings often produce a pair of units, creating four-car trains.

No. 150221, 20 August 1998

No. 150221 is seen at Plymouth carrying Regional Railways livery. This platform at Plymouth is usually used for the Gunnislake services. The letter 'P' on the front of the unit indicates that this is the end where the parcels bay is fitted.

No. 150221, 2 June 2000

No. 150221 is seen still working in the West Country, this time at Exeter St David's with a working to Cardiff Central. No. 150221 still carries Regional Railways livery, but the logos have been replaced with Wessex Trains logos.

No. 150222, 1 April 2008

No. 150222 stands on the buffer stops at Liverpool Lime Street. The unit still carries the former First North Western stars livery. Northern still operates twenty-eight members of Class 150/2.

No. 150223, 24 June 2008

No. 150223 departs from Manchester Piccadilly, having recently been repainted into Northern Rail livery. The unit is on a working to Sheffield.

No. 150224, 26 December 1989

No. 150224 spends Christmas 1989 stabled at Tyseley carriage sidings. The unit still retains its Sprinter livery in which it was delivered from BREL York a couple of years previously.

No. 150225, 15 June 2017

No. 150225 stands at Leeds, having just arrived with a terminating Northern working. This is another example of the class that wore 'Welcome to Yorkshire' logos on the bodyside.

No. 150226, 30 December 2016

No. 150226 is seen at Manchester Victoria with a Northern working to Wigan Wallgate. This unit was transferred to Northern from London Midland, where it had been disbanded to form three-car units, Nos 150008 and 150013, in the West Midlands. It was reformed into its proper set when it moved north. It had been disbanded for twenty years.

No. 150227, 24 August 2005

No. 150227 is seen at Hampton-in-Arden while working a local stopping service from Coventry to Birmingham New Street. It was unusual to see diesel units working on this route due to their slow acceleration. The unit carries former Anglia livery, but has Central Trains logos added to the ends of the carriage. It was named *Sir Alf Ramsey* when in use with Anglia.

No. 150227, 4 August 2018

No. 150227 is seen arriving at Cardiff Queen Street carrying unbranded Arriva Trains Wales livery. In October 2018 this unit would pass to Transport for Wales, which has inherited the thirty-six members of the Class 150/2 fleet from Arriva Trains Wales and is the largest operator of the sub-class.

No. 150228, 13 August 2004

No. 150228 departs from Doncaster with an Arriva Trains Northern working to Sheffield. It had been seven years since privatisation, but this unit still retained Regional Railways livery, complete with a large Arriva logo.

No. 150228, 24 June 2008

No. 150228 arrives at Manchester Victoria with a terminating Northern Rail working. This unit now carries an earlier version of the Northern Rail livery on which the lines were more angular, the later livery having more rounded edges to the stripes.

No. 150229, 18 June 1990

No. 150229 arrives at Crewe with a Regional Railways working from Derby. Of note is the fact that the unit doesn't carry a deflector plate on the front to protect the wheels from obstructions. It later passed to Anglia, where it was named *George Borrow*.

No. 150230, 1 June 2000

No. 150230 is seen at a busy Exeter St David's in company with classmate No. 150233 and another unidentified member of the class. All three units still retain Regional Railways livery, but with Wessex Trains logos. No. 150230 later carried the name *The Tamar Kingfisher* when repainted into Wessex Trains livery.

No. 150231, 22 February 2017

No. 150231 is seen arriving at Manchester Piccadilly with an Arriva Trains Wales working to Holyhead. The Welsh-based Class 150/2 units occasionally visit Manchester but are not as common as their Northern counterparts. This unit had previously been operating for Anglia, where it was named *King Edmund*.

No. 150232, 1 April 2002

No. 150232 is seen at Plymouth with a Wessex Trains working through to Cardiff Central. This view shows the Wessex Trains logos off nicely, covering up the old Regional Railways branding. This unit later gained the name *The Coastal Connection*.

No. 150232, 14 April 2016

No. 150232 arrives at Bristol Temple Meads carrying Great Western Railway green livery. This was one of the first Class 150/2 units to carry this livery, which looks good on the units, especially with the GWR logo on the gangway door.

No. 150233, 13 January 2016

No. 150233 is also seen arriving at Bristol Temple Meads, this time with a working to Weston-super-Mare. This unit carries First Great Western 'dynamic blocks' livery, with the white, magenta and blue lines made up of place names along the Great Western route. When in Wessex livery this carried the name *The Lady Margaret of Looe Valley*.

No. 150234, 9 May 2000

No. 150234 departs from Plymouth with a Wessex Trains working to Cardiff Central. Note the former Rail Express Systems parcels stock in the background, with Plymouth being a very busy hub for such traffic at the time. This unit was later named *The National Trust*.

No. 150235, 12 May 2001

No. 150235 stands at Lowestoft with an Anglia Railways working to Ipswich. At the time, this unit carried the name *Cardinal Wolsey*; it would be transferred to Central Trains in exchange for a Class 156. It was later transferred to Wessex Trains, where it was named *The Falmouth Flyer*.

No. 150236, 11 October 2005

No. 150236 *The Lord Clinton* is seen arriving at Southampton Central carrying Wessex Trains livery. The livery of maroon with pink doors was certainly distinctive, and No. 150236 is working towards Portsmouth Harbour, a duty today undertaken by Great Western Railway Class 158 units.

No. 150236, 4 August 2018

No. 150236 is seen making a station call at Cardiff Queen Street carrying Arriva Trains Wales livery. It was heading for Treherbert and is now operated by Transport for Wales.

No. 150237, 27 March 1993

No. 150237 departs from Crewe, carrying recently applied Regional Railways livery, heading for Nottingham. Today these services are operated by East Midlands Trains using single-car Class 153 units. No. 150237 would later pass to Anglia Railways, and would be named *Hereward the Wake*.

No. 150237, 30 July 2016

No. 150237 stands in Platform 0 at Cardiff Central with an Arriva Trains Wales working to Ebbw Vale. This platform was added to increase capacity at this busy station.

No. 150238, 1 August 2002

No. 150238 stands at Exeter St David's with a Wessex Trains working to Exmouth. Today this unit can still be found on such workings as part of the Great Western Railway fleet. No. 150238 would later receive the name *The Exeter Explorer*.

No. 150239, 22 May 2008

No. 150239 is seen at Bristol Temple Meads carrying recently applied First Great Western 'dynamic blocks' livery. This livery was very novel and showed the pride that FGW had in its local links.

No. 150240, 30 July 2016

No. 150240 rolls into Cheltenham Spa with a terminating Arriva Trains Wales working from Maesteg. The Arriva Trains Wales livery suited this class of unit.

No. 150241, 26 December 1989

No. 150241 is seen on Tyseley, having been split into individual cars. No. 52241 would be inserted into No. 150148 and No. 57241 would be inserted into No. 150149, to make un-renumbered three-car units. The Class 08 behind is No. 08920, a long-term Midlands-based shunter.

No. 150241, 9 August 1992

No. 150241 is seen a couple of years after the previous photograph and, as can be seen, it is back together in its original formation and was photographed rounding the curve past St Blazey, heading towards Par from Newquay. It later carried the name *The Tarka Belle*.

No. 150242, 14 December 2016

No. 150242 is seen arriving at Cardiff Central with an Arriva Trains Wales service to Aberdare. The whole class is currently going through a refurbishment programme, making it compatible with current PRM (People with Restricted Mobility) regulations.

No. 150243, 22 May 2008

No. 150243 arrives at Bristol Temple Meads with a Great Western Railway working to Plymouth. The set still retains its attractive Wessex Trains livery, which included West Country advertising. Wessex Trains had been absorbed into the Great Western franchise in 2006. This unit once carried the name *The Filton Partnership*.

No. 150244, 21 April 1987

No. 150244 is seen departing from Leeds, having not long been released for service from BREL York. In the background can be seen the parcels sidings, which have since been redeveloped into extra passenger platforms. This unit later carried the name *The West Cornwall Experience* when working for Wessex Trains.

No. 150245, 2 September 1995

No. 150245 is seen at Glasgow Queen Street carrying Regional Railways livery, but with Scotrail branding on the blue stripe. Scotrail operated eighteen members of the class north of the border, but they were reallocated to Arriva Trains Wales in 2005.

No. 150246, 26 May 2004

No. 150246 is seen at Newquay, waiting to depart for Plymouth. This set carries Wessex Trains livery, which certainly looked quite bright on the class. Today, No. 150246 is still operating in the West Country, but for Great Western Railway.

No. 150247, 14 April 2016

No. 150247 is seen stabled at Bristol Temple Meads in between duties. This was one of the first members of the class to receive Great Western Railway green livery, which suits the class well.

No. 150247, 30 July 2016

No. 150247 arrives at Cheltenham Spa carrying Great Western Railway green livery. It will go into the siding north of the station, and then return to take up service towards Swindon.

No. 150248, 22 May 2008

No. 150248 departs from Bristol Temple Meads carrying Wessex Trains livery. This unit also carried the name *The Great Gardens of Cornwall*, and the plate can be seen on the right-hand carriage, underneath the first saloon window. Wessex Trains operated twenty-five members of the class, which were all absorbed by Great Western Railway.

No. 150248, 22 October 2016

No. 150248 is seen stabled at Goodrington Sands sidings, carrying Great Western Railway green livery. These sidings are just outside Paignton station, and this view was taken from a passing steam-hauled working on the Dartmouth Steam Railway.

No. 150249, 3 July 2017

No. 150249 is seen on the final approach to Bristol Temple Meads with a Great Western Railway working to Exeter St David's. The unit still retains its First Great Western 'dynamic blocks' livery but would soon lose it in favour of GWR green. This previously carried the name *J. Charles Lang*.

No. 150250, 4 August 2018

No. 150250 arrives at Cardiff Central with an Arriva Trains Wales working to Newport. The unit had lost its Arriva branding by this point and would transfer to Transport for Wales operation in October 2018.

No. 150251, 12 June 2008

No. 150251 is seen waiting to depart from Crewe with an Arriva Trains Wales working to Chester. The unit is seen carrying the original Arriva livery, which would be replaced by a darker blue livery.

No. 150252, 4 November 2018

No. 150252 awaits departure time from a very wet Cardiff Central with a Transport for Wales working through to Ebbw Vale.

No. 150253, 17 November 2008

No. 150253 arrives at Cardiff Central, carrying the original Arriva Trains livery, with a working through to Penarth. Transport for Wales has thirty-six members of the Class 150/2 available for service and is the largest operator of the sub-class. This unit had previously carried the name *The Exmouth Avocet* when working for Wessex Trains.

No. 150254, 5 July 1999

No. 150254 arrives at Totnes with a Wessex Trains working from Plymouth to Cardiff Central. The unit carries former Regional Railways livery, but with Wessex Trains branding, and has just descended Rattery Bank, which is over 4 miles long, into the station.

No. 150255, 30 July 2016

No. 150255 is seen having arrived at Cardiff Central with a terminating Arriva Trains Wales working. In this view, the unit still retains its Arriva branding, which is bilingual. It was named *Henry Blogg* when it was based in Norwich working for Anglia Railways.

No. 150256, 17 November 2008

No. 150256 departs from Cardiff Central carrying the original Arriva Trains Wales livery. The unit is operating to Pontypridd; South Wales has been associated with the Class 150/2 units for over thirty years.

No. 150257, 30 July 2016

No. 150257 is seen having arrived at Barry Island with a terminating Arriva Trains Wales working and will soon depart for Merthyr Tydfil; Barry Island is the interchange station for the Barry Island Railway. No. 150257 carried the name *Queen Boadicea* when it was operated by Anglia Railways.

No. 150258, 31 August 1996

No. 150258 is seen arriving at Edinburgh Waverley with a terminating Scotrail working. The class was used on Fife Circle duties north of the border, but also visited Dundee, Stirling and Dunblane.

No. 150259, 2 September 1995

No. 150259 stands on the buffer stops at Glasgow Queen Street having arrived with a terminating service. As can be seen, the unit carries Regional Railways livery, but with Scotrail markings, including one on the cab front.

No. 150259, 30 July 2016

No. 150259 arrives at Lydney, carrying the original Arriva Trains Wales livery, with a working from Cheltenham Spa through to Maesteg via Cardiff Central.

No. 150260, 13 August 2013

No. 150260 departs from Cardiff Central while working towards Penarth. The Class 150/2 fleet in South Wales is due to be replaced with new stock from 2023 onwards, but in the meantime it is being refurbished to a high standard.

No. 150261, 13 August 2013

No. 150261 is seen arriving at a very sunny Cardiff Central station with a Great Western Railway working to Taunton. The 'dynamic block' livery it's carrying would soon be replaced. There are currently no plans to replace the Class 150/2 in the GWR fleet. While working for Wessex Trains, this unit carried the name *The Riviera Flyer*.

No. 150261, 3 July 2017

No. 150261 is seen at Bristol Temple Meads having been repainted out of its previous livery and into plain blue. The unit is seen carrying the name *The Tarka Line: The First 25 Years 1989-2014*. It has since lost the name and has been repainted into GWR green livery.

No. 150262, 24 June 2008

No. 150262 awaits departure time from Crewe with an Arriva Trains Wales working through to Manchester Piccadilly.

No. 150263, 13 January 2016

No. 150263 arrives at Bristol Temple Meads with a Great Western Railway working from Weymouth. The Weymouth services are occasionally worked by a pair of Class 150/2s. This unit once carried the name *The Castles of Cornwall*.

No. 150263, 18 June 2019

No. 150263 is seen stabled at Exeter St David's after the individual cars have been split from each other. This view shows the couplings between the two carriages: a simple bar coupling. Also, note the tail lamp fitted. This car is No. 57263.

No. 150264, 14 December 2016

No. 150264 departs from Cardiff Central with an Arriva Trains Wales working to Penarth. Out of the eighty-five two-car Class 150/2 sets delivered from BREL York, just two have been withdrawn, both due to collision damage, with the two good cars from each set being coupled to make a workable set. No. 150264 previously carried the name *The Falmouth Flyer*.

No. 150265, 22 October 2016

No. 150265 departs from Paignton station, travelling over the busy level crossing just off the end of the platforms. The unit is working a Great Western Railway service to Exmouth via Exeter St David's. It was once named *The Whitley Wonder* while carrying Wessex Trains livery.

No. 150266, 14 December 2016

No. 150266 is seen at Cardiff Central with a Great Western Railway working to Taunton. The GWR examples are not as common visitors to Cardiff as the Transport for Wales examples.

No. 150267, 28 May 2000

No. 150267 is seen having just departed from Par station with a Wessex Trains working to Newquay. The unit is just passing the site of St Blazey Depot, which is still in use today, operated by DB Cargo.

No. 150268, 14 September 1995

No. 150268 arrives at Cardiff Central while still carrying Sprinter livery. This unit was part of a large batch of Class 150/2s that were allocated to Cardiff Canton for use in Wales, but they were all transferred to Northern. This unit was named *Benny Rothman – The Manchester Rambler* in 2007.

No. 150269, 4 June 2013

No. 150269 stands on the buffer stops at Leeds, in part of the station that used to be the parcels area. This unit started life in South Wales, before transfer to Northern.

No. 150270, 4 August 1996

No. 150270 leads a pair of Class 150/2 units as they are stabled for the weekend at Rhymney. A Class 143 Pacer unit can also be seen to the right. Today, some of the peak-time services are in the hands of Class 37 locomotives with Mark II carriages through to Rhymney.

No. 150271, 4 June 2013

No. 150271 is seen having arrived at Leeds with a terminating Northern Rail working. Note the East Coast-liveried Mark IV carriage in the background, another type of train synonymous with the railways of West Yorkshire.

No. 150272, 9 June 2016

No. 150272 departs from Manchester Piccadilly, heading for Hazel Grove. The unit carries Northern Rail livery but this is complimented by adverts for the blues festival in Colne.

No. 150273, 16 July 2013

No. 150273 awaits departure time at Leeds with a Northern Rail working through to Harrogate. The unit carries Northern Rail livery but is one of quite a few members of the class to have had 'Welcome to Yorkshire' adverts added. This once carried the name *Driver John Axon G.C.*

No. 150274, 22 February 2017

No. 150274 stands at Manchester Victoria with a Northern working. This is another Class 150/2 to carry 'Welcome to Yorkshire' adverts and, as can be seen, the adverts came in many different colours. Most have now lost the adverts, with the majority of the Class 150/2 units now carrying Northern white livery.

No. 150275, 16 June 2017

No. 150275 is seen arriving at Manchester Piccadilly. This was the first member of the Class 150/2 fleet to be repainted into the bright Northern white livery. It also has the light clusters painted yellow rather than the usual black. This unit has since been named *The Yorkshire Regiment – Yorkshire Warrior*.

No. 150276, 13 April 2016

No. 150276 arrives at Manchester Piccadilly with a Northern working from Rose Hill. This is another member of the class to carry 'Welcome to Yorkshire' adverts, this time in turquoise.

No. 150277, 22 August 2016

No. 150277 stands at Leeds, having just arrived with a terminating Northern working. This time the 'Welcome to Yorkshire' adverts are in green.

No. 150278, 14 December 2016

No. 150278 makes a station call at Cardiff Queen Street carrying Arriva Trains Wales livery, complete with branding. The unit is seen working though to Barry Island and will call next at Cardiff Central.

No. 150279, 4 August 2018

No. 150279 departs from a very sunny Cardiff Queen Street with an Arriva Trains Wales working through to Barry Island. The Class 150 units were built to carry nearly 150 people seated and are ideally suited to the Valley lines in South Wales.

No. 150280, 21 September 1995

No. 150280 departs from Manchester Piccadilly carrying a very clean Regional Railways livery. The class helped to eliminate first-generation DMUs from the areas they served, mainly Manchester, Leeds and the South West. This unit would later carry the bilingual name of *University of Glamorgan/Prifysgol Morgannwg*.

No. 150281, 14 September 1995

No. 150281 arrives at Cardiff Central carrying Regional Railways livery with a working to Treherbert. The South Wales-based examples were based at nearby Cardiff Canton, and still are today.

No. 150282, 13 August 2013

No. 150282 arrives at Cardiff Central with an Arriva Trains Wales working to Merthyr Tydfil. The unit carries the old version of Arriva livery, but also has a 6G shed code underneath the running number, which indicated Llandudno Junction in North Wales.

No. 150283, 12 June 2008

No. 150283 leads a pair of Class 150/2 units at Crewe, both carrying the first version of Arriva Trains Wales livery. No. 150283 started life north of the border, based at Haymarket, but transferred south to join the Arriva fleet in 2005.

No. 150284, 14 December 2016

No. 150284 arrives at a cold and damp Cardiff Queen Street with an Arriva Trains Wales working through to Penarth. This was another former Haymarket-based Class 150/2 that migrated down to Cardiff in 2005.

Nos 150285 and 150228, 12 October 1994

Nos 150285 and 150228 are seen side by side at Edinburgh Waverley. Both units carry Regional Railways livery, complete with Scotrail branding, and both are on Bathgate workings. These units would have different career paths upon leaving Scotland, with No. 150285 heading to Wales to work for Arriva Trains Wales, while No. 150228 headed to Manchester and now works for Northern. No. 150285 would later receive the name *Edinburgh–Bathgate 1986–1996*.

No. 150921, 13 August 2013

No. 150921 arrives at Bristol Temple Meads with a First Great Western working from Great Malvern. This three-car set was made up of the two cars from No. 150121, with car No. 57212 inserted. It only ran for a short while before the centre car was removed and put into set No. 150126, with No. 150921 reverting to the number 150121.

No. 150925, 14 April 2016

No. 150925 is seen departing from Bristol Temple Meads. This is another hybrid set, this time with car No. 57209 added to Class 150 No. 150125. The three-car sets were renumbered into the 150/9 number series by First Great Western. The set has since been disbanded, with No. 150125 returning to its normal formation and transferring to Northern. No. 150925 can be seen carrying the name *The Heart of Wessex Line*.

No. 150926, 13 January 2016

No. 150926 is seen at Bristol Temple Meads, running as a three-car unit. The centre car is No. 57212, which has since been removed and paired with car No. 57209 to form set No. 150209. All the Great Western-based sets have now been transferred to Northern.

No. 150927, 13 August 2013

No. 150927 is seen at Cardiff Central with a First Great Western working to Taunton. This was set No. 150127 with car No. 57209 added, but it only ran for a short while before it was removed and placed into unit No. 150125.

No. 154001, 13 May 1987

No. 154001 is seen passing Saltley Depot, Birmingham, on its way towards New Street. This was delivered as three-car Class 150 No. 150002 but was renumbered for test purposes. Note the extra boxes on the roof, which were later removed. It was later renumbered 154002 and ran temporarily as a two-car set until October 1987, when car No. 55401 was reinserted.

No. 154001, 31 May 1987

No. 154001 is seen on display at Coalville open day, 1987. At the time, this was formed of just two cars, with the centre car removed. The set was renumbered from 150002 and was used to trial equipment that would be fitted to the Class 158 Express units. It was later renumbered 154002.

No. 154002, 23 February 1988

No. 154002 is seen passing Washwood Heath as a three-car set. This was built as Class 150 No. 150002 but had its Perkins engine replaced with a Cummins power unit and was fitted out with a Class 158 interior. It later reverted to a standard Class 150 and was renumbered back to 150002.

Nos 999600 and 999601, 10 August 1988

Nos 999600 and 999601 are seen arriving at Leeds. This was a special Class 150 unit that was built as a test unit. It was built in 1987 by BREL at York and followed on from the end of the Class 150/1 production run. It has only ever been used by the British Rail Research Division, later passing to Network Rail. This is the livery the unit was delivered in: grey and light blue with a red stripe with the designation 'Mobile Test Assessment' on the red stripe.

Nos 999600 and 999601, 24 October 1996

Nos 999600 and 999601 are seen again at Leeds, eight years after the previous photograph. In the intervening years the unit has been repainted, with the light blue area giving way to dark blue. The unit is used as a track-recording vehicle and can be seen working the length and breadth of the country.

Nos 999601 and 999600, 7 April 2014

Nos 999601 and 999600 are seen approaching Bescot Stadium from the direction of Walsall at Pleck. As can be seen, the unit now carries Network Rail yellow livery and has been fitted with video cameras on the front as well as other recording equipment. Its livery has since been further changed with the addition of various Track Recording Unit logos.